through the
prism of time

(poems on love, hope, journeys)

through the
prism of time

(poems on love, hope, journeys)

Rita Malhotra

HAWK PRESS

Published by

Hawk Press
4836/24, Ansari Road, Daryaganj
New Delhi – 110 002
Phones : 9643330713, +91-11-23278618, +91-11-35676207
E-mail: thehawkpress@gmail.com
www.thehawkpress.com

dedicated to my loving family

"Poetry is the language in which man explores his own amazement".

—Christopher Fry

Introduction

The book Poetic Pictures and Picturesque Poems stand testimony to the epigram

The poems are a thousand pictures

The pictures are a thousand poems

The collected poems in this Selection are on a wide ranging issues, seen through the prism of a mathematician bringing together the binary perspectives of Life and Death, of Hope and Despair, of Agony and Ecstasy, of Timeless travel to Borders and Beyond, of Screaming Victims and of the Shouting Ignited Woman. Packed into four sections they offer a glimmer of hope to sagging spirits devastated by the visitation of once in a hundred years pandemic, to the rise of dawn after dusk, to the lovers at times distant, at times close. The poems further offer a glimpse of the land of Gods to the souls caught up in the landscape of life and the prospect of emancipation for a Molki from her incarceration within brutish desires. The poet trapped in the endless chaos of life's ebb and flow rises like the phoenix to light from darkness, to creation from destruction, to Paradise Regained from Paradise Lost.

— Dr. Hema Raghavan

Eminent Author, Former Dean University of Delhi and Principal Gargi College, University of Delhi.

Author's note

The present book is just another milestone in my poetic odyssey for it is still a long way to the final destination and I believe that one lifetime is not enough to reach the same. It has however been an elevating experience at every step of this journey. My fascination with poetry began as a young adolescent with reading poetry, that soon became a passion and over time as I discovered its magically transformative power, it slowly metamorphosed into my soulmate. In my struggle to keep myself whole in this faceless world, its obstinate constraints, to retain my identity in Hardy's madding crowd and perhaps to move away from the sameness of diurnal existence, I began penning my own lines. Both have played a significant role in assimilating the world around me as well as other cultural gestures. Poetry has also gifted me with a beautiful meditative space of solace and peace away from the vortex of life's complexities.

A confession now about the fact that I have never been able to constraint my inner anger and protest at the social evil of the exploitation of the girl-child and women in general. In fact, one path that I followed in my quest for inner peace was to give an honest voice to my protest. That compelled me to dedicate a separate section in this book to a woman's journey. My sensitive conscience orders my poetic sense and sometimes a pure and raw emotion creates its own space in my verse.

Also, as an advocate of one of the truest perceptions of human life and the emblem of a timeless world, I was compelled to bring 'love' under the parasol of a separate segment. The recent pandemic has already carved a significant space in History and the accompanying perils changed the very fabric of our lives. That entailed a dedicated space to those dark moments of our everyday existence and constitutes another separate module. Global travels as invited delegate to writers' conferences and poetry meets, triggered the travel poems and personal experiences of plural hues of life comprise the concluding section.

Acknowledgement

First and foremost, grateful thanks and profound gratitude to Dr. Hema Raghavan, a stalwart of English literature for understanding my passion for poetry. Her encouraging words have always given me the desired fillip to continue composing in this genre. Her patient reading of the poems in this collection and the subsequent introduction to the book are so much to be grateful for.

My heartful sense of obligation to eminent poets Ambassador Amarendra Khatua, Poet and Former Diplomat Blaine Marchand, French Writer and Poet Rolf Doppenberg and all the literary luminaries for penning such kind words about my writings.

I have always received invaluable support and immense love from noted poet-friends Ms. Mandira Ghosh and Ms. Sanjula Sharma for their often-appreciative opinions on my humble achievements in the realm of poetry.

I am in complete debt of words when it comes to my family for bearing with me through my constant demands for time and attention, especially to Ashok and Kunal who gave me immense support through my never-ending problems stemming from my limited e-literacy.

Grateful thanks to my passionate publisher for her courage to publish a text that is far removed from the category of popular writing, in this day and age of instant gratification.

Sincere thanks to my young friend Mr. Aamir Ali for his contribution towards giving the right shape and structure to the contents of this book and for the cover design. His honest advice has always been welcome.

Appreciative indebtedness are due to my translators, earlier publishers and editors of literary journals and anthologies for placing their trust in me and including my work in their esteemed publications. A resounding shout-out to all of them.

A special word of gratefulness for my interviewers on Prasar Bharati and the print media. Their regular invites and inclusion of my poems in their programmes and columns have helped me evolve in the literary realm.

With the kind of perpetual and tremendous encouragement that I have been fortunate to receive from multiple quarters, I hope to pen many more acknowledgements in future.

Contents

Section III
travel poems

Section IV
womanhood across social wilds

Section V
landscape of life

SECTION I

as times turn dark
poems on the pandemic

1.

connect
(a tribute to our courageous medical professionals)

the five elements conspire
to assault my senses
with that lethal, invisible nemesis
each agonizing breath borrows
a minuscule puff of oxygen
as i enter the township of solitude
nameless
they remain masked, calm
faceless

yet we connect deep-
in my desire to cherish, those
outlying undreamt dreams
and their humble urgency
to shield a choking soul
from the fangs of Yama*
doctor and patient follow
time's footsteps into
the elated intersection
of life's Venn Diagram

we connect in our hopes
(hopes are not wayfarers,
they have a destination)
my focused hope to heal
a fragmented consciousness and
theirs to lend that sanguine glow
to yet another dying flame

we connect in our aspirations-
mine to see them conquered
in fulfilment-smiles
(Orpheus takes the path from light to dark
and back to light)
theirs to watch my exhilaration
in victory-lined eyes

when gasping breaths first met them,
when hopes were but a sea of ash,
i was merely a COVID number
they, the summoned saviours
strangers-in-arms then,
we are soulmates now

we connect in our optimisms
in a two-star constellation
draped in the same dreams,
we battle the same foe
hum congruent hopes
we breathe synonymous desires

we connect in our goodbye gestures-
their plural palms in farewell cheer
my folded hands, grateful tears

their nests woven in my heart,
i say a silent prayer

outside-
an artfully-attired careful scape
in singular poise, in dainty pace
inhales deep, the
ethereal, mystical, morning-mist.

---

*In Hinduism, Yama, also referred to as Yamaraja, a Rigvedic deity, is the Lord of death and justice. In the Puranas, Yama is depicted as having four arms, protruding fangs, and the complexion of storm-clouds with an expression of wrath.

2.

let's keep the music on

fear-tethered unity across maps
bereft of dots
resonates in unmatched grace
virtual synergy in cyberspace
as the virus rages on
kindred tears, parallel dreams
remain dressed in their formal best
defying black holes of the times
to keep the music on

promulgation, communication
from sanitized sites of seclusion
from bondages of quarantine
death in a hurry, whirlpools of misery
outsides clad in ghost-shadows
(Goya's dead escape from his dark paintings)
but the insides, in meditative chants
keep the music on

Vishnu* beseeched, Indra invoked
earth rechristened hell
seas silenced, skies smothered
the sun limps on crutches of shadows
as the universe measures
its memory's depth
in recall of moribund songs
of the savage grippe espagnole**
yet raga bageshri*** meanders in
to keep the music on

heavens wrapped in grey shrouds
muzzled beaks of singing larks
thoughts circle broken mirrors
a brutal history carves itself
on the city's crimson, throbbing face
yet, that infinitesimal spark of hope
eludes the ferocity of furies unknown
to keep the music on

the wrinkled man whispers love
to moist eyes of an age-bent wife
"tears too have dreams" he says
the third eye of the westward sky
has its own tale to tell---
homeward birds are flying in
with loving, distant folks and kin
to keep the music on

past water-rapids and forest-shades
anticipation in green embrace
wings its way to earth's door--
the rare orchid will bloom once more

herons will fly the sky in flocks
gentle zephyrs would sing again
to keep the music on

who says
melodies are extinct?

---

*Known as the preserver, Lord Vishnu is one of three supreme Hindu
deities. Vishnu's role is to protect humans and to restore order to the
world. Indra, in Hindu mythology is the king of gods.
**The Spanish flu of 1918
***Raga Bageshri is a Hindustani classical raga. It is a melody that
pleases in isolation and is effective in emotional expression.

3.

blurred lines

(in tribute to Late Dr Kaul who left us aggrieved fighting his battle against COVID)

today i can only pen silence
as our poet-mate steps into
the oblivion of ethereal eternity
time stands stone-still
myriad thoughts permeate
the flakes of reminiscences
to fill sad, empty spaces of reality
between sun and anti-sun
between moon and anti-moon
with everlasting, remembrance lines.

nature's metaphysical canvas, captures
the guardian angel's broken wing
devastated hibiscus blooms, collapse
like soap bubbles
notes of Beethoven's moving symphony-
the funeral cantata, drift in with
the sensed, yet hardly-felt, stoic breeze

in the chorus of a thousand prayers
a million memories in poetic drape
rise to moist, tranquil eyes
then diffuse into the purple brilliance
of a peaceful, new awakening--
a timeless evolution
for the imperishable soul.

4.

death is no longer
lighter than life

sacred memories, solemn goodbyes
woven in sandalwood sticks
customarily lend, a sense of
profoundness, to the fragrant pyre
soaked in whirlpools of emotions

father's last arduous breath
in bondage of an appalling chaos
absent palms cannot calm his torment
as the merciless, invisible foe
watches unshaken, the
soaring COVID-count

baba always wished to sleep
with the mountains
but today, his soul cries alone
on the stoic stack of wood
mourning his disconnect with nature

untouchable moist words reach out
from beneath the listless heap
but lose their grasp of the tangible
father lies in restless stillness
Helios* limps on crutches of shadows

mother's agonised eyes by the
grieving window, contemplate
baba's garden-family in deep distress
tearful, agitated nasturtiums
shrivelling jasmines, impassive pastels

absent hymns, mute mantras
no offerings to ancestors or gods
no marigold wreaths or fragrant petals,
the burning pyre whispers regrets
and shuffled memories, to shielded ears
of masked men, metres apart
time rock-still, in its bewildered frame

death of a poem
death of a song

auspicious sandalwood pyres
are a fragrant mélange of histories
a source of past's ashes
that depict the immortal soul
and adorn Shiva's forehead
Shiva, the emblem of destruction
of the fear of death

but today, the cobweb of alien times
engulfs history

angry flames on the hissing heap
destined to annihilate and burn
play the wicked assassin

the ash is no longer sacred
the pyre confined to a mere square
on mother's moist digital screen
as a trembling, flickering
farewell-candle bids a last adieu
how can such an unpardonable death
ever remain lighter than life?

---

*Helios: Greek Sun God

5.

spring

a tiny poetry-cart
enters the lazy township of words
on wheels of time
scattered, sleepy words
still in lockdown mode
strangers to each other

poetry coaxes, cajoles
and befriends them
capricious words wake up
from dreams
turn decisive and traverse
the invisible walls of distance
to converge at a happy reunion
"allow us a voice" they say
and join the train of reflections
a touch of magic
as the poetry-lamp is lighted

poems pen new desires
and melodies of the soul

on a fresh page of thoughts
the township rejoices
in the spring-time harvest
of the new virus-nullifier
(they call it the vaccine)
the township also rejoices in
the garden-fresh green harvest
of embryonic nascent poems

the petite poetry-cart
in elegant gait, in patient pace
transforms into a caravan.

6.

time too has an oasis

they manufactured death today
in a state-of-the-art lab
called it 'black devil' the famished raptor
that ravages in malignant manipulations

Artemis* at our threshold
humankind captive in time's frozen frame
unable to dream the form of a flower
in metaphysical skyward gaze
sighs at universes beyond, their lucent suns
and illumined stars in anticipation
of cupping their moons in eager palms

handcuffed deities in sanitised shrines
echo an uncanny, surreal silence
myth nor mystery can light a lamp
tomorrows lurk in agony
questions spark tearful tales
shadows, just a memory

'black devil' on the garden fence
orchid-clusters, withering-roses
in blue autumn isolation,
strive hard to withhold colour
a subtle hint of sweet fragrance

cuckoos' carols melancholic
empty rustle of pensive leaves

do jasmines ever blossom in death-land?

'black devil' in hot pursuit
city-dreams in smithereens
pallor stretched across the skies
Rabia the frail adolescent
mother's callused palms in hers,
trudges dazed through dust and haże
homeless, bleeding, migrant feet
on sun-rained, rugged, grey concrete
till dusk turns the corner

where are the pathfinders to promised lands?

a shadow theme to these throbbing words
assuages the restless, perturbed soul--
history's witness that crafted rogues
only live their carnage in sacred lands
where cosmic rays fall like gems
where plural gods in unison
choreograph the ascent of stars
craft smiles of wistful moons
(liquid notes of Beethoven's moonlight sonata float in)
where nights wake up from dreamless sleep
to hopes draped in morning mist
where, time too, has an oasis.

---

*Artemis, in Greek religion is the Goddess of hunting, of wild animals
etc. Armed with a bow, quiver, and arrows, she sends plague and
death among mankind and animals.

7.

indebted

(tribute to the men in uniform on COVID frontlines)

i cruise the ocean of
my inner being seeking truth
in painful, predestined realities
in spaces where the sun has
forgotten to rise
where light does not illuminate
do I even deserve to pen poems-
i ask of myself, while
the insane, invisible rogue microbe
carves days with savage force
claws its way into innocent mortals
sunk deep in lonesome worlds?

dried roses, shrivelling jasmines
arid haystacks of thoughts
contemplate its lethal force
as the vulpine virus obliges
gasping beings in tedious breaths
to long for relief in painless death
to pray for burials dignified
for composed, vedic funerals

alas! the die is loaded heavy
against these feeble, helpless humans
as Gods stay mute in stoic shrines

but, braver gods in human guise-
surface in a phoenix rise
their third eye in constant vigil
our valiant selfless forces arrive
putting to shame the cunning foe
wiping trails of raw despair
helping shift the mist of gloom
shoving aside, all grieving thoughts
kindling love, kindling hope

the last lines of this nascent poem
proud of our men in uniform
shower petals of gratitude
watch relieved, those winged blossoms
like fairies plucked from the sky
watch moonlit graves, trace miles of smiles
watch light-waves mirrored in rainbow-skies

a million souls in synchronised cheer
rise in beholden gestures
for our angelic, deific, golden men
as the panchabhuta drape themselves
in subtle carnation-redolence

indebtedness springs from enlightened souls
they bow in prayers to be born again
in the safe cradle of our warriors dear
on fragrant earth in sun or rain.

SECTION II

through the prism of love

8.

in the queen's land - Ranikhet

*love looks not with the eyes, but with the mind-and therefore is
winged cupid painted blind.*

—Shakespeare in 'A Midsummer Night's Dream'

flanked by quiet
the rage of rains falls calm
eyes assimilate
sights and sounds
of cloud-kissing curves
of narrow winding concrete
along green-ochre slopes

eternal realm
of a shining stream
affirms the beauty
of scarlet flames
in hillside blooms
in the wall-clinging concoction
of white and pink rose-bushes

at the mist-draped glass pane
of the dream house
high up in brume-laden hills
the silhouette of shy lips
celebrates their fullness
fingers entwined in trembling touch,
eyes locked in wordless silence,
plural cupids* frolic
on the decorative renaissance
art-piece in the background

a fragile love shivers through
darkness rituals
ticking moments slowly gather
the savoured moments
to weave them into
dream-studded tomorrows.

---

*Cupid continued to be a popular figure in the Middle Ages, when under Christian influence he often had a dual nature as heavenly and earthly love. Multiple Cupids frolicking in art are the decorative manifestation of proliferating loves and desires.

9.

desire

deluging desire waits
in shadows of a smile
beginningless, endless
disquieting beauty- angelic
lilac skin-fragility of butterfly wings
she is darkness
for you to sprawl upon
waiting
for the not-yet-born
kiss

10.

beyond reason

corridors of darkness
your hesitant touch meanders
through stray pathways
every street celebrates
every corner weaves a story

night slowly fades
around a handful of stars
the amorphous horizon
of wild unreason touches reality

in love's arms
amongst cradle-rocked rhythms
sleep soothes the ransacked body
i seek refuge in the haven
of beautiful dreams
i do not look for a reason.

11.

unmasked

she let him traverse
the mind's corridors
unchecked to shape
destiny's smile

nascence of new buds
lavender fragrance
of new blossom
new harmony

moonstruck, they strum
the monsoon strings
passion's gushing rivers
cascade into
heaving oceans within

infinity crystallized in the momentary!

kissing his way
into a welcoming world
he assimilates love

given in frenzied earnestness
as if time will never return

love's horizon sculpted!

but alas an arc from
the horizon's arch, breaks away
the mask drops
unable to harbour
dead fragrance any longer
her quivering countenance
drowns in grieving time's
torrent of tears

today she does not even trust
her own shadow.

12.

void

---

carefree as a tender leaf
i remained curled around your love
in unwavering fidelity
in unwavering trust
you inhabited my dreams as Adonis
i remained your coy Venus
together we set galaxies on fire
i viewed the world through your eyes
as you did through mine

i often played Radha
in Krishna's divine halo
the whiff of jasmine
mingled with the twilight breeze
at every street crescent, moonlight
remained the face of cupid
skies descended to our doorstep
but today
pushed into exile
in my lonely web-world,
i spread your vows, your earnest words

across the open virtual chessboard
promises kept on white squares
broken ones on black
blacks outnumber the whites
perhaps always did
but my third eye remained shut
to time's shifting strategy
in declaring a checkmate

as images float in
from rewinding frames
i see a life lived
only behind a perennial mask.

13.

storm

love trembles
breasts burn in autumnal passion
seraphic glow on lily face
she traverses night's untrodden lanes
through raging storms
across paths blazing in the dark
through songs of wild winds
and changing melodies
of the night breeze

through the curtain of darkness
a shy dawn smiles
light falls in soft showers
carnations open petals
fragrance of a promise fills the air.

14.

in the arms of a *ghazal

❧❦❧

in the exquisite pain of love
every word searches
for your pure presence
every note on your flute
mingles with the musk
of lingering lines of my verse

sprawled in the arms of a ghazal
we build spaces
for passion's play
warmth of touch trembles
today i am the queen on a chessboard

history gushes past
forgotten love-stories
pushed over the edge of the universe

void, illusion and absence
metamorphose into
the continuum of your presence

outstretched arms
of the mild twilight hour
reach out to embrace
a shy moon rising out of
the star-strewn lake-mirror

content in our world
of velvet thoughts
of simple realities
we feel closer
to the essence of ghazals.

---

* The ghazal is a poetic form comprising rhyming couplets and a refrain, with each line sharing the same meter. It may be understood as a poetic expression of both the pain of loss as well as the beauty of love in spite of that pain.

15.

let the sun be late this morning

come, plunder my body
drown me in ocean-deep desire
make me a slave of frenzied passion
explore labyrinthine alleys with
magic tremors of touch
light a lamp at every street-corner

a panting sky watches
the stars drape themselves
in colours of envy,
fingers of darkness linger
in sacred folds, in sanctified depths
on their way to the hallowed shrine

tumultuous tempest
titanic upheavals of seismic passion
from kiss to kiss we taste
pleasures of paradise
earnest, unharnessed bodies
move in synchrony
with mridangam beats of rapture

the night burns itself out
in trying to deflect the flame
of burning lips
stars fall to cinders
time lingers heavy
a dazed sky continues to graze along
pastures of still-hungry desires

two souls pray in unison-
let the sun be late again this morning.

16.

agony

dusk, twilight
alone
on the empty
expectant bed

every night
the dream
goes up in flames.

17.

chrysanthemums

we were brought up
by the rule book
that spelt love for us daughters
as immoral, infidel,
masked, contagious
dreams were cached
within constrained confines
the self, remained dwarfed-
bonsai like
unable to reach beyond its grasp
but a moment of wild defiance
unleashed a tempestuous will
to self-expression
i followed love's trail
scanning the horizon of darkness
to arrive at the moonlit patch
of a perplexed night-
a night that witnessed
love's intimate dance
in the sensual celebration of
intimacy between

soul, mind and body
with the first footfall of dawn
i tore all pages
of the book of norms
made paper-flowers out of them
this morning they have metamorphosed
into golden-orange chrysanthemums.

18.

twin sun

across the canvas
on the mind's easel
brush-strokes paint
the absent soulmate's presence
in hope-filled, intimate hues

a hundred virtual doors
stand open, mirage like
your silhouette steps in
to close the distance

i do not let colours fade
from the creases in my silken spaces

days end-

i rest my head
on the pillow of peace
sunset dreams tread centuries
desire lights up the night
stars watch in envy

till the mist of dawn
arrives at my open window
a smiling cloud on its shoulder

i shake awake a blinking dawn
sunflower golds, turn their heads
in invocation to a twin sun
to a new sunrise.

19.

pain

mask of night
threads of darkness
crisscrossed on
the mind's canvas
fragments of memory
from distant yesterdays
return--truth laden
pain laden
temple flowers wither.

20.

let me remain the ignited woman

together we crossed
boundaries of love
night after intense nights
yet with surreal timing
you broke the nest of fidelity

entangled in a mesh
of disillusionment
i burrow through tunnels of time
gather fragments of broken dreams
and pile them up on the pyre
of now-dry memories

in the rising funeral flame
i realize that
time will not change its habits

sitting by the open window of my mind
i watch the green sapling
that i planted at

the corner of my heart
its beauty lies in its response
to the still-alive remnants of love

light and dark of life disclosed,
i untie the knot of emptiness
to tread the path of love again
every end they say,
has an everlasting beginning
so i take an eternal pledge
to remain
the spirited, enduring, ignited woman.

_21._

images

bound together
by those lost moments
of togetherness
and the not-so-lost-ones
we versify life
bathed in its
beautiful sufferings.

22.

torrent

soul-stirring, withered metaphors,
fall silent
*yellow carnations and
sagging nervous leaves
remember those bygone springs
of passion-filled yesterdays
now frozen cold like
the kiss of dead lips
as the soul masters the art
of shedding tears
sun-faded, disillusioned dahlias
wait in agony
for the angry torrent within
to calm down, wait in agony for
gods to concur with Cupid and Venus
wait in anticipation of the
pacific smiles of autumn fragrance
wait for the wisdom of winter
for tomorrow's vibrant hues
of yet another spring.

---

* yellow carnations symbolize disappointment or rejection.

23.

*Jewish Bride by Rembrrandt

bound together
destiny in expressive anticipation
cherished fusion of the pious and
spiritual
in love's tender touch
Rembrandt's canvas flashes past

splendid pearls, luxurious
oriental robes and a shy smile in
'The Jewish bride'
the Old Testament comes alive
ephemeral thoughts drift past
the intimate moments in the embrace
of Abraham and Sarah,
of Boaz and Ruth,
of Isaac and Rebekah.

---

*The Jewish Bride is a painting by Dutch painter Rembrandt, painted
around 1665-1669.

24.
*The Kiss by Gustav Klimt

aureate, resplendent, entwined--
depiction of a passionate unvoiced
embrace in
the gleaming honest perspective of
a deep human emotion, in
the art nouveau style
of Gustav Klimt's 'The Kiss'
reality in a dream or

dream in reality?
let us light golden candles
to the divine communion
in the land of infinity
in the land of Orpheus and Eurydice.

---

*The Kiss is an oil-on-canvas painting with added gold leaf, silver and
platinum by the Austrian Symbolist painter Gustav Klimt.

25.

Le Printemps
by Pierre-Auguste Cot

under a canopy of green
colours sing romance
locked in the intense fervour of
a dynamic, seismic love
eyes in a playful swing-embrace
flowing robes exude

rainbow-nuances of emotions
the red, his burning desire
the pristine white,
her dove-soft innocence
as the artist brings to life
the elements on his canvas,
in " Le Printemps"
the scape bursts into a love song.

---

*Le Printemps (Springtime) is a mid-19th century painting by French artist Pierre Auguste Cot. . Done in oil on canvas, the painting is currently in the collection of the Metropolitan Museum of Art.

26.

*The Kiss by Francesco Hayez

secret passionate kiss
the fire in the crusader's rich maroon
complements the calm, fresh, flowing blue
of the captivating enchantress
spell of bewitching magic woven in the nest
of the artist's imagination
a perfected Italian Renaissance
in a nuanced play of filtered light
and enigmatic shadows
in the capture of raging romanticism
a timeless, phenomenal level of realism
remarkable, radiant, ravishing.

---

* The Kiss (Il Bacio) is an 1859 painting by the Italian artist Francesco
Hayez. It is possibly his best-known work.

27.

*The Honeysuckle Bower
by Peter Paul Rubens

time and space forgotten under
the arching honeysuckle bower
--a symbol of love
light hues and lightness of being,

metaphors of an everlasting union
in the blooming buds of love

the bower shelters the embrace
of two enraptured souls
inundated in tenderness
the sword-holding chivalrous protector
the fragile yet confident demoiselle
newly espoused

deluge of hope, of contentment
in two expressive pairs of equanimous eyes
cultural devotion in traditional attires
all converge to an endless perpetuity
a cherished permanence as
love shakes hands with eternity.

---

*The Honeysuckle Bower is a 1609 self-portrait of the Flemish Baroque painter Peter Paul Rubens and his first wife Isabella Bran. They wed shortly after he had returned to the city after eight years in Italy.

28.
*Danse à la Campagne
by Pierre Auguste Renoir

elegance of Renoir in the
consciousness of the supreme truth
in the dynamics of emotions
with romance as mainstay
illuminating their time

poetry in the pause!

his eyes behold
her dainty self in white gossamer
her love-stricken smile
effervescence of melody in her eyes
the ladle of desire begins to stir
an iconic dream sequence anticipating
the yet-unformed kiss.

---

* Dance in the Country (French: Danse à la campagne) is an 1883 oil
painting by French artist Pierre-Auguste Renoir. It is currently kept at
the Musée d'Orsay.

29.

*The Lovers
by Rene Magritte

in that gestural abstraction
of the shrouded mystery-kiss
do we spot a cached passion
a lightning strike in the touch of lips
or souls shedding tears?

with a sense of frustration
in unrequited love

emotions seem unsettling as
in the weeping willow tree
why the obscurity?
is her pale face, a waning moon
behind the grey of the hood
or is she wearing a vibrant smile
is he in despair like half-dead sprouts
or radiating a full-lipped smile?

as thoughts walk to the rainbow's end
i see a derset hue on the shoreline
an erotic fire aflame within.

---

*a 1928 painting by Belgian artist Rene Magritte

30.

A Stroll on the Canal at Quimperle
by Henri Le Sidaner

mesmerizing subtle beauty
of the enigmatic, almost mysterious nature
rhythms of soft romance
and whispers of silence
in the shimmering aura of nascent love

a bucolic feel in the classic
impressionist style
lit up in vibrant yet nuanced hues
reaches out to art lovers
the amorphous crepuscule hour
sculpted by the radiating moonlight
water ripples illumined
and intense love-thoughts of the two souls
eavesdropping on themselves
evoke intimate tranquil moments
that feel like a whiff of jasmine
in the silken twilight breeze.

---

*Henri Le Sidaner was a French-Mauritian painter

SECTION III

travel poems

31.

history in flames
(Notre Dame, Paris 2019)

treacherous, leaping flames pave
the highway to cloud chambers
the iconic spire sighs heavy
then succumbs
the powerless parisian seized by
a sense of profound loss
watches in sheer disbelief
the tall majestic architectural marvel
collapse like a storm-mangled pole

denizens of the city of romance chant
cry and pray in
the spiritual dislocation
as times past and present surge by
nineteenth-century images of the
crowning of Napoleon
the liberation of Paris
times surge by images of
Charles de Gaulle attending mass
of Victor Hugo's immortalization of
the cathedral
memory of a collective inheritance--
today the enchanting edifice is veiled
in ash and debris

i am non-Christian, non-French
non-European,
i am simply a fellow mortal

once an inhabitant of the
fashion-city with innumerable dreams
etched in an ambitious demeanour
yet I too was horror-struck at the
heaving images
of the handsome testament--
a symbol of peace, of a civilisation
today shrouded in despair

dazed millionaires in sacred solidarity
donate in units of millions
for history to remember that
their generation rebuilt
the memorable icon of deep affection
but a nagging question haunts the mind-
is preserving past inheritance
the question brulante or saving
fellow-humans from heinous forces
cloaked in ruthless chill of killer icicles?

the Charlie Hebdo massacre abrades the senses

i hold onto the three-decade young picture
of the resounding structure
towering behind me
Christ smiles a second good bye as
ferocious yet reluctant flames
mask the magnificent metaphor
of the superlative
the soul of Paris continues to burn
i suffer continued assaults on memories

two tear-drops remain perched
on frozen lashes
dementia seems my only solace
the flames continue to rise higher.

32.

Chicago cycle 1

brushstrokes of words
on the mind's week-end canvas
weave their own story
a radiant sun rests deep in thoughts
rhymes waltz on the champagne sparkle
of endless, transparent waters
arms stretch out to touch the skies
rhythms shine off, dove-white sail boats
an endless queue of blushing tulips--
chins raised high
run riot in flaming colours
the intense fragrance
permeates the summer breeze

fluidity of feminine desire!

islands of green tranquility
dot the city-scape
grey-black intense, intricate sculptures
evoke soulful emotions
at once intimate and universal

in a surreal world with me, mine
and my snatched meditation
i remain in alice's wonderland.

33.

Chicago cycle 2

sanctity of the city-canvas
changes stance
language changes face
as high-rises interrupt
the virgin scape
binaries of identity step in
with the inverted glory
of the drone and groan of
helicopter-hoardings floating
in virgin air above Lake Michigan
above faceless names and
nameless faces.

a synthesis of human hues
black, brown, white
bustles past the social complexity
on breathless yet stoic sidewalks
that breathe a life of their own
as men and women beckon at passers-by
with "homeless, please help" placards
around their necks

magic returns with the deepening dusk
when rain embers of fireworks
rise up the navy pier
enhancing the fairytale skyline and
holding a mirror to this historical city

night tiptoes into
the dense architecture of dreams
as i watch a new dawn
prepare to keep pace with
the fresh beats of Chicago rhythms
history rises with a purpose
Swami Vivekananda's voice resonates
harmony, proclaims peace
on common grounds of religious unity
with the doctrines of Bhagvad Gita
wherein, every path converges to
the abode of the almighty
Chicago sanctified, gives a feeling
of the timeless
Chicago whispers--union with the divine!

34.

Chicago cycle 3

what is divine, what divinity
but the perception of
the warmth of movement
in one's vicinity
Keat's autumn comes to mind
with the season of mist
and mellow fruitfulness-
an approximation of divinity
perhaps
for, behind that autumn-countenance
lurks a cruel Chicago winter
furious winds wait in ambush
as nature slips its lyrical beauty, its
affable apparel, off its shoulders
on lonesome streets, sculpted across
the *schizophrenic city scape
thoughts stumble on rocky terrain
emotions tread the opposite path
their relation, a mere delusion

when winds find time to slumber awhile
emptiness fills the chilled spaces
under a frozen sun
memories fall unconscious
buried beneath shrouds of snow
stoic-still towering trees, resemble
the white chalk-cliffs of Sussex
loneliness falls into heavy debt of words

not enough cause for panic they say
for the divine is not too far away
nor is divinity
both will come with another spring
Chicago summer will usher them in
the essence of movement will return
perception of human fragrance
fill all immediate spaces

as tulips beat the winds away
as petals glaze in golden rays
as providence steps in yet again
crowned in its halo of divinity
Chicago smiles a beaming smile.

35.

landing at Dallas

a beautiful mirage in the play of light
on the grey shroud of
an untrodden stretch
captivates the soul
clouds careen into light showers
cotton hills watch over the baby-drops

a limping sun on crutches of shadows
strains its mind hard for
a strategy to flood yellow
the unambitious, uninitiated sky,
a sky within my grasp, yet so far
a surface-calm winding river
slithers snake-like, on white terrain
from miles above in wonderment
i gauge the mood of silver waters

the descent begins with the slow ascent
of the toy-town of Dallas
keeping pace with the approaching runway
rows of mud-patches on fenced playground

perhaps for the falling raindrops,
are brown wedges on green carpet
a serene silence is all i capture

tiny reds, blacks, yellows race past
on two-inch wide lanes
bikini-clad barbie dolls splash into
a slowly expanding mini turquoise pool
all so gloriously picturesque
seemingly chiseled by a skilled sculptor
the exquisite beauty of minimalism

but history disturbed
the mind is soon caught in
a whirlpool of emotions
relics of John F Kennedy step in
the riding presidential motorcade
gun shots shake the senses
to a seismic, sanguinary impact
goddess of illusion betrays,
yet once more
the past trots a furious pace
to intrude upon the present

as wheels touch ground,
the self, shakes hands with
realities, both beautiful and cruel
with the present as with bygones
with changing faces, changing hues
of each uncertain today
of each uncertain tomorrow.

36.

land of the gods

the timeless consciousness of Benaras
is awakened by the mist-clad goddess of dawn
in tiptoeing steps like a deer in the dark
to resume her walk in light.

a peaceful, pious morning
opens its eyes from a dreamless sleep, its
listening eye assimilates the ethereal notes
of morning ragas, of enduring melodies
in the soft lull of ripples
across the enigmatic, enchantress
the incessantly flowing ganges
draped in silent shades of silver gossamer

benares embodies
the deepest mysteries of humanity
encapsulates ageless traditions
epitomizes vedic rituals
captures the laws of mythology
in divine chants of the mangala aarti

invoking Lord Vishveshwara--
ruler of the universe

times past and present flash by
the river-lined city
carving history across ancient by-lanes

in naïve wide-eyed innocence
the city's sentience gazes in awe
at the spiritual, mystical shimmers as
sun-goddess stretches the waters
to contemplate her golden face
the essence of life runs relentless
through the auspicious flowing expanse
flower-adorned diyas* smile in
floating salutations to the gods

the city's beguiling soul now assumes
a shifting stance
as it walks past burning funeral ghats
ghats that never sleep
yet allow nights and days to slumber deep
ghats blazing in flames immortal
ghats veiled in shrouds of smoke
black oblivion, their only halo

today through chants of holy hymns
shabed kirtans, the dawn-azan
and temple chimes
i fulfil a loved one's last wish at
the solemn yet charismatic
manikarnika ghat

i watch his human form cross
the gateway to life beyond

today i wave my last goodbye
to a doting father
adorned in white jasmine-fragrance
on his chosen journey to moksha
as i pen what i know of a stunned silence
in this mythical city--the site of my solitude

today i trace the path of the lone grey kite
sailing the firmament as baba
wearing his soft memory-smile
remains a face in the rising moon.

37.

disconnect
*(*Mumbai 26/11)*

dazzling spotlights
enhance velvet-skin
on chiseled faces and
bare shoulders
shapely legs in needle steps
walk the ramp
modern meets the ultra-modern
in manufactured beauty
(Aphrodite shapes a sanctimonious smile)
fashion walks through decades and styles
smiles assembled to hypnotize
state-of-the-art cameras
in a hallucinatory world
a world that claims continuity
with the real world outside,
even as transient fashion statements
inside, shut out the sinister fire of
violence outside - consequence of
a warped ideology, as
the meaningless business of gunshots
holds Mumbai, to ruthless ransom

disrupting an elegant era
today, only red oozes out of
the cracked soul of the city

reality forgets its signature
puzzled lines on its forehead
try to discern
between inside and outside
between the reality of illusion
and the barbaric starkness
of dehumanising actuality
as screams of innocent hostages
drown in silent echoes

outside, fear haunts the phantom city
like an invisible monster
steel gestures of ruthless maniacs
outwit Poseidon and Neptune
stealthily touching land by the sea route
spreading the virus of hate
tomorrow's newspapers
prepare to scream death yet again
Mumbai remains the face of tragedy.

disconnect personified in the
rolling cameras
that resume their focus on
the next aspiring, sculpted model.

---

*The 2008 Mumbai attacks (also referred to as 26/11) were a series of terrorist attacks. About 174 people died, including nine attackers with more than 300 wounded.

38.

moon-showers (Tajmahal)

a stir a shift, a feeble tug
wing flutters within
a note, a tune, a symphony
an echo of love within

i commune with the past
history complies
love's frantic pulse
races past
the throbbing confident
moon-blessed marble
legends revolve around the
the motif magic that
splashes plural colours
on the canvas of thoughts
desire envelopes like
a wave with no horizon

eyes behold the smiling stars
tears of ecstasy mingle with
golden-silver showers

time watches in wordless wonder
as love-birds on silver wings
reach pinnacles of rapture

dawn descends smiling shy
to lift the cloud of mist
to rock the radiant dew
across miles of buried memories
i traverse endless boundaries of
cherished passion
as death continues to celebrate
the flow of life
the flow of love.

39.

" *Shiva's silence* "
(the 2013 Uttarakhand disaster)

noon image
futility of a clinging sun
on the breast of a shamed, helpless sky
the exquisite architecture
of the Kedarnath Shrine
tracing centuries of mythology
warms to yellow
yet we hear no echo that recalls
rhythms of life

Shiva, the bestower of longevity
trapped the descending Ganges
in his matted locks, absorbing her fall
yet today, he thrust the Mandakini down
from the high trapeze of ruthless glaciers
washing villages off the map dragging
scarlet remains of annihilated beings
that belong to the river now

Shiva played the conventional destroyer
oblivious to the difference between

beautiful and ugly
between man and ghost
between life and death
he watched the tandav of nature
as the debris at the temple threshold
gathered heaps of bones, bodies and
vestiges of life
are these merely cultural delusions
for Shiva the supreme hermit?

a vertiginous night descends
sad lights on the mountain scape
rise out of blackened waters
the cadence of darkness is mine alone today
i sit to write the countless forgotten names
in my remembrance diary
uncertain thoughts ask of the
lone survivor, the shiv-linga*
why is life so short
why is death so long?

---

*Shiva linga is an abstract or an iconic representation of the Hindu
deity, Shiva, used for worship in temples, smaller shrines, or as self-
manifested natural objects.

40.

jugalbandi in the Niagra Falls

jugalbandi* of emotions evoked
in the thundering roar of deafening
seemingly destructive waters
hues of blue, green, white and silver
relentlessly fall off the shoulders
of the mesmerising falls
speaking an extravagant language

paradise descends on aqua green
to bless the sun-nourished rainbow
floating on dancing waves
another paradise rises
in a spray of pristine mist
permeating the cool, crisp air
in rhythms oblivious to
the powerful pace, the drumming beats
of breath-taking cascades, a sight
that beholds all senses
in the jugalbandi of thunder and silence

beauty in power!
power in beauty!

Shiva's spectacular Tandava comes alive
in jugalbandi with Parvati's Lasya**
thoughts of the oneness of creation
and the divine, surge through
fathomless depths of the adbhuta

in an over-riding sensation of ecstasy
time trots a furious pace
yet time stands still
effervescence of captivating melody
resonates through the soul
releasing it from illusions of suffering
both time and space experience
the stupendous, the sublime
in perfect jugalbandi

adbhuta in the cosmic canvas of nature
adbhuta in the real yet surreal
as every moment discovers
new creativity, new eternity
new infinities.

---

*The term Jugalbandi originated in regard to Indian Classical Music
and is about being on an equal footing.
**Lasya is the dance performed by Goddess Parvati expressing
happiness in its grace and beauty. In the context of Hindu mythology,
she is believed to have danced the Lasya in response to the male
energy of Tandava, the cosmic dance performed by Lord Shiva.

SECTION IV

womanhood across social wilds

41.

molki
(for a male heir)

sold from village to village
man to man
it is business as usual--
carnal pleasure betrays
the play of emotions
as, the primate in every "him"
grazes along pastures of blind lust

time has crossed over to
the other side of reason
emptiness circles her huddled self
by the dying wood-fire amidst
acrid smoke and garbage stench

the body is her only sin
every inch under the scanner
the soul torn out of her being
she is labelled a molki, a paro
a trafficked bride for a male heir
religion of benevolence shamed
another history subsumed in its rubic

steps into a retrograde phase

the visceral anxiety for her little girls
born four in a row, traps her in
the cobweb of misplaced notions
the virus plays no role here
only primeval convictions thrive
in heavy debt of compassion
in the overflowing urn of gloom

was that really the Shiva-Linga**
she worshipped from girlhood
to womanhood
or merely a piece of rock? else
why would those intense prayers
for a Shiva-like husband
lead her to the wolves' den?
in her silent pain, is heard
a soul-wrenching call
"Draupadi*** i beg you
to circumscribe me".

Call her paro or a molki
her only mask is the metaphorical
burqa of primal fear
as days sink in deep despair,
haunting visions of phantom nights
leave brutal scars
on the skin of a mortified sun
on skies shrouded in grey monochrome

a stranger
even to the ground she treads upon,

her mute screams of protest
drown in voiceless echoes
drown in the deep abyss
of a menacing, dark silence
dissipate, in seismic tremors
of an alien time
tomorrows trace a question mark.

42.

ma

the horizon bends down
to usher in her mystical power
the ultimate reality
Ma Durga descends from beyond
the endless canvas of blue
attired in symbols of the
divine powers of Vishnu, Varuna, Vayu
Surya, Yama, Indra, Shiva and Agni
eager conch-shells sound the clarion-call
rejuvenated gardens turn verdant

strains of ragas in twilight-gait
curate shared cultures of the east
in the sway of tiny flames
as a thousand earthen-lamps
glow in gay abandon!

Ma's shakti-smile
casts a spell in shades of grace
chorus of worship-chants
infuses the aura with durga-spirit

ma's eternal consciousness
rains trishuls, rains tridents
on prowling asuras in human guise
dark forces succumb to divinity
in the collapse of mahishasura-
the reveler in chaos, in anarchy
who raves in turning heavens to hell.

time walks past earth-rotations
to arrive at vijayadashami's open doors
ma sheds her earthly drape
vermillion-smeared devotees wearing
tears and smiles, bid adieu with
farewell offerings
Ma returns home across the seven seas
in an air-water-wind-woven drape
paradise departs with her.

in an earnest wish to turn back time
we beseech you--come back ma
the earth would have no misery then
no misogyny, no nirbhayas
no heart-wrenching screams of
brutalized Asifas*, no child-woman's ashes
no graves in lonely cemeteries

henceforth, every poem of mine Ma
would only be a hushed invocation
a silent prayer.

---

*8-year-old Asifa Bano of Rasana village near Kathua in Jammu and
Kashmir was abducted, gang-raped and murdered, in January 2018.
An outrage followed and the culprits convicted.

43.

leela is sixteen

a year limps by in nano steps
as leela the widow
remains a prisoner
in the messy, confined core
of everyday struggle
carrying the burden
of invaded virginity
and ostracization
leela the widow turns 16 today
in a faded white attire

the customary tears
dried up long ago
when destiny deceived
dazed emotions lost colour
through sinking sensations
on the painfully pious bridal night
when her glass-shattering shrieks
broke the consciousness
of the unity of her being
when oozing red, spread its
slow tentacles to engulf

the fragments
of kaleidoscopic glass bangles
her dream-bangles
leela the widow turned sixteen today

as the candle of life
burns at both ends
leela continues to remain
the distorted face of tragedy
her silence has no secrets
monsoons do not sing
broken stories pile up
into heaps
of abuse and abandon
as leela the widow turns sixteen today

44.

honour

the lone temple-bell chimes
chants of the priest's mantras bless
the emotional exchange of garlands
his moist eyes absorb the unsure
semi-smile on her quivering lips
assimilate her supple innocence
draped in coarse red cotton

she had blossomed in time's crevices
a lotus in the all-consuming quagmire
of regressive, rural kin when
fate arrived like a blazing breeze
riding on his handsome shoulders
she became his fragile secret, the
sparkle in his eyes, the effervescence of
happy, humming songs on his lips
like Radha was on Krishna's flute
luxury of dreams would be theirs now
nights would walk in glowing light

but the phantom of caste
hurled its brutal shadow

of the inverted glory of illogic
to deform love, to deface it
"traitor" screamed the kin
protector parents turned predators
she had disgraced the family honour
for his God was different from hers

in organic fear the moon slipped behind
menacing black clouds, that engulfed
and trampled the pious bridal night.

the first ray of dawn shuts its eyes
in shock, in scarlet shame as
two inert victims of senseless perception,
of steel gestures, lie sprawled red at
the village crossing
victims of a ghastly, brazen defiance
of the truest universal emotion

soul-wrenching voices rise in protest
for the two young buds yet to blossom
even as they wonder--aren't we stars of
that one single constellation of castes
called magnanimity or is it humanity?

why coin caste-names, caste-hierarchies?
why let songs turn into distorted echos,
let honour be dishonored?
why should tomorrows suffocate in death-fogs?

the never-ending trail of questions continues
the relentless quest for answers continues.

45.

emancipation

dawn dusts away the stars
a calm moist breeze rustles past
wet sun beams, past gold-streaked
ocean-waters

her now tranquil self
inhales the freedom fragrance
she watches shark-smooth hems
in the turquoise drape
of earnest, waltzing waves
coconut palms queued up
along the shore
bend double in green silence

at the threshold of this subliminal plane
she pledges not to shudder at
each passing wind
in controlled quiet, she removes
her bangles--fetters of the past
one by one like dry scabs
of an old wound
her escape from the dark cavern

of brutal animal desires
is legitimized today

stepping out of darkness
in freedom-gait, head held high
she is transformed to colour, to fragrance
to become that rare carnation
monsoon bursts into a radiant love song.

46.

daughter

you came like a
drift of sunshine
in continuation of our
togetherness
on a spirited morning
the air came alive
in jasmine vibrance
winged angels showered smiles
skies burst into a song

the twilight hour in firefly glow,
stars draped in sparkling gold
the world transformed to
a fairy-tale land as we rejoiced
in your glittering allure
shimmering eyes, gossamer feel
and screams of glee
carefree as a tender leaf
you remain a rare orchid in
life's garden

God's miracle-gift!

time assimilates its fragments
into your passionate self
embellishes my oyster with
the beauty of calligraphy
you are present
in every poem of mine
in melodies of the tunes, we hum

may you traverse endless realms
of cherished passions
across time, painted in tulip hues
may rhythms of life remain alive
dawns descend in pearls of dew
may rainbows illumine your days
mornings wake in *harsingar breeze
may, nights dance in dainty dreams

you my child, are an ode
to silver moons and golden stars.

---

* harsingar or night jasmine is a small ornamental tree that has
fragrant white flowers with orange twigs.

47.

towards infinity

on black canvas
larger and deeper
than its geometric measure
she lights the stars
one by one
paths of light and dark
cross in much more
than Kant's perceptions
of time and space

on canvas
in her journey of self-discovery
through absent colours of love,
realization dawns that
time will not change its habits.
she splashes the black patches
with golden hues, then
lights the pyre
of now-dry memories
dark, now emerges as a source of light

on the illuminated canvas
she recreates
the cosmic scape of nature
she joins broken pieces
of the horizon
to obstruct the reckless
volatile celestial forces
from crucifying earth's flesh

on the lighted canvas
she embarks upon
a journey to the absolute
seeking salvation from
the cycle of birth-rebirth

in her sublime union with
transcendence
she crosses eternity
seeking redemption
seeking moksha.

48.

gift

i carry a lighted candle
through a small window
of time, to kindle life within
nine months later
as a sleepy sun seeks refuge
in night's embrace
i travel through my body to reach you
i live each breath of yours
you are the reflected rainbow
in the prism of my eyes

through winding tributaries
of blood conduits, i race to keep pace
with the flow of my blood
your blood
i shiver through each contraction
of my proud womb
their finer movements converge
in your tiny being

in the creases of smiling thoughts
i live a secret dream with you
sharing unspoken words
i turn the needles of my clock
for dawn to slip in early
and weave tomorrow's face

magic in your first cry
in response to the call of the world
the river of love gushes out
incarnation of the vatsalya rasa
in touching you, i touch the face of God

as dawn descends the morning path
a twin sun awakens in our shared space
alongside the diurnal morning star.

49.

grandma smiles

weather-beaten walls come alive
framed memories reflect
leaping images of rich yesterdays
shadows from the past sneak in
through tapestries, time-worn
brocades, lack lustre
and skeletons of rose petals
on the old teak console

the wheel of time turns
sad strings of the dust-washed *sitar
yearn for those magic fingers
musical notes of the **asavari raga
resonate, echo and re-echo
(granny seemed to have the blessings of the ***Mousai)
thoughts ride waves of emotions
as granny's luminous eyes
smile through her death-disguise.

---

* The sitar is a plucked stringed instrument, originating from the Indian subcontinent, used in Hindustani classical music.
**asavari is a Hindustani classical raga. It belongs to the Asavari thaat and is performed in the morning hours.
*** The MOUSAI (Muses) were the goddesses of music, song and dance, and the source of inspiration to poets.

50.

colours

i dared to play god today
i created the pastel-blue sky
on canvas
poured casks of light on it,
chose rainbow hues
the silver air too
seemed to adorn itself
in lingering light and
jasmine fragrance

i held back the greys of past's return
i kept at bay my sense
of limited vision
of colourless days
and dark tomorrows

i then turned around
to borrow colours
from the sparkling mirror
of my lover's eyes
from the infinity of other mirrors
around me

i adjust the easel, pick up my brush
but alas, I paint only
blacks, blues and purples.

51.

i remain an open window

how many summers
do i remain open as
winds blow hot, blow cold
into this ghost house of absence?

images move in like hungry hawks
tear open the insides only to
move out in sunset thoughts
in homeward flight

in ruthless gesture they walk in
announcing the death of moons
satiated, they move out
the window now opened wider
desires coagulate on their way
from dreams to nightmares.

if only i could down the shutters
if only i could raise a wall

grenades of male sharpness
fly in unabashed

and pierce through my consciousness
i watch helpless
the pile of shrapnels rise
yet remain the mute chiseled window
linking outside to inside

an innocent destiny remains grilled
to concrete walls
of the ghost-house of absence
if only i could pen verse
if only i could write a song.

52.

only twelve or all of twelve?

she is only twelve they say
a half-open lotus bloom
too innocent to be watchful enough
of her little brother
too young to be present at
post-dinner discussions
for nine o'clock is her time for bed

yet when those unwanted days arrive
month after month
they tell her that she is all of twelve
she is old enough to keep at bay
overtures of male cousins, old uncles
and prowling eyes at school or play
wise enough to avoid gleeful screams
through those sky-touching swing-rides
and games of hide and seek

when afternoons sleep undisturbed
the guileless child in her
and the nascent child-woman
in illusions of similarity

tiptoe out of the children's room
for the daily ritual of
asking her mirror-image
in intense simplicity
"am I only twelve or all of twelve?"

53.

light at the caste-window

obstinate bars confine
her existence
screams soaked in silent echoes
pierce the soul, nightmare-like
bent beneath the deadweight
of caste
she chokes on her dark tedium

tortured verbs make up
the hammered patchwork
of thoughts
dreamless tears bleed memories
into the crevices of time
through each ticking moment
she waits for those dried-up springs
to flow again

as seasons advance
through their unending cycle,
she manoeuvres cliff-edges of grief
reason limps into her consciousness
a vacant gaze metamorphoses
into searching eyes
new threads of thought
combat confinement in caste's prison
the self unwrites myths of history
lending light to the embryo of
a casteless dawn.

SECTION V

landscape of life

54.

paper boat

her burgled house is a township of stupor
every inch ransacked, in distress
hinges hang off branded almirahs
their doors agape in shocked trauma
like shoed horses
tears race down the tributaries of
her wrinkles, as a void conscience
permeates her stoic self

afloat on violated spaces
heaps of strewn papers--former
inhabitants of passive drawers and safes
of boxes in cosy corners and concealed nooks
papers tinged yellow, some ink-stained
others fresh and crisp, handwritten, printed
stir her listless coffee with memories

buried postcards, illegible signatures
candles alight on festival cards
faded notes of student days, paper bags
Tagore's songs and music lessons
in the old maroon diary
nursery rhymes, fairy tales,

adolescent verse in company
love-letters sneaking out
of newfound freedom-doors
papers in all shapes and shades
scribbled confessions by her child
in discoloured, disfigured diaries
reveal the culprit of that broken vase
from her fine-crystal collection
forgotten years elide into
the present moment, yet smiles elude her

vivid reminiscences fly past, through
a dazed deluge in memory-lane
consciousness dawns that
recaptures are more treasured, than
missing pearls and silverware
or gold wedding bracelets

gathering and gluing the faded recalls
she configures a paper-boat
thoughts often set sail on it
in the hope of touching port
at remembrance-regions

can blissful oblivion dwell in
infringed spaces too? perhaps yes
for time is the magic healer
today her paper boat is safely anchored
as she rests peaceful
in the haven of sweet reminiscences.

55.

good bye YouTube

the self all set to shed the kilos
with YouTube-assured remedies
waits impatient as the yellow
ad-line touches destination
the request to press the bell-icon
and video-share now complete

we banish belly fat in ten days
says an aptly-attired dietician
you'll walk the ramp in needle steps
a fortnight is all you need
excitement rides the winds
i see myself as
the spring-collection show-stopper

sparkle with apple-cider shine
bid farewell to statin drugs
(my doctor couldn't be wrong, could he?)
early morning aloevera juice
and the heart will never betray
the gleeful green-gourd is next
and hypertension scurries away
add healthy yellow and zesty orange
salads will add that sunshine glow
the avocado-march past the screen
cleanses the stomach, the liver, the spleen

kidneys pulsate at optimal pace
white garlic enhances grace
one cinnamon stick will do the trick
confident claims for a youthful face
magic potions in cyberspace
distorted joints back to shape

all ailments gone, yet chaos rules
fuzzy diffusions in
colour-constellations
test the kinetics of thoughts
doctors rendered redundant
reeling thoughts in a tizzy
my nerve centre hollow and oh so dizzy
is all askance, about the fate
of Darwin's cargo of genes as
i return once more to the screen

in store are more doctorless cures
clueless i am, and confused
but the YouTube host smiles in triumph
leaving me and my cluttered brain
featureless as desert terrains
the mind veiled in a shroud of fog
what'll happen to my rainbow pills?

thank you, web world for the food galore
i shall perhaps return for so much more
but for now and for sure
between ultra-violet and infra-red
i swallow the capsules in a row
adding health for life's flow
for the ultra-female virtual glow
sorry YouTube for your zero score.

56.

friend eternal?

my last poems perched
on a rippling serene scape
in a gold-bordered frame
smile adieu from the study-wall

i quiver in excited anticipation
to greet a new friend
i have often longed for
in the spaces of my silence

she shall fly across skies
cut her way through winds
thunder and rain, past distant dunes
to liberate me from throes of
anger, hurt, pain, desires
to liberate me from male codes
to snap cords of conceit and pride
my remorse quotient shall touch
a perfect shoonya, they say

thoughts revolve in anticipation
would she be shy and withdrawn
or spirited and intense

would i find rose bushes in bloom
and frangipani fragrance
in her much-spoken-of angelic abode?

a soft knock on my door
i step out draped in ageless tradition
fresh white sari, white jasmines
adorning my hair
vermillion in my parting
scarlet bindi on the forehead
my willing hand in hers
we depart for my dream-sojourn

what is your name dear friend, i ask
smiling, she replies .
"since the moment of my birth
i have been a child of silence
solitude's been my only friend
parents call me death, my dear"
her steel gaze pierced in time
a flash of lightning, a revelation
blurred lines, ink blue darkness
the final curtain as life recedes
i float in black oblivion.

57.

game

we first met over a game of chess
a common passion turned into
an everyday-ritual
coffee accompanied the moves
both trivial and complex
most evenings I won
he smiled away his defeats

evenings turned late
coffee-time ran into pre-dinner drinks
dinner often followed
his was the first move
that stormy evening
as he shoved aside the checkered board

night stammered through shivers of touch
and flushed trembling lips
reason took a backseat despite
my feminine grace
i became a willing chessboard
every move belonged to him

he overshot legitimate paths
in earnestness for short cuts

to declare the final check-mate
my thoughts ran a frantic search
through pages of history of
this complex game
for a clever counter-strategy
but failed
a sharp satirical thrust said it all

today in my first defeat
i had perhaps lost forever
he turned over, smiling his first victory.

58.

the soul discovers its eternity

in continuous thoughts
the mind becomes an opaque screen
imprisoned in the world of shapes, of forms
else it's engaged in the consciousness of
the unmanifested, the beyond

but

in walking with nature
my mind honours that rapturous realm
absorbed to the brim
leaving no space for its mental habit
of labelling

a tranquil wave of freedom sweeps over me
stillness echoes laughter of the winds
silence screams ecstasy
to the grace of the mighty mountains
in a glorious burst of white
the sun-kissing peaks reflect expressive colours
the mind's eye moves across
the compelling canvas
to suit its parameters of art and beauty

the walk with nature continues

in the immeasurable, infinite umbrella of blue
the upward gaze connects
with diverse philosophical strands
the silent core of the being
discovers romance
in penning these lines and
bows its head to the elements

earth, water, air, fire and space
symbols of birth, re-birth, life, death
nostalgia and joy
the soul in its metaphorical journey of love
discovers happiness in its own eternity.

59.

partition (1947)

crippling acts of treason
reason lost in the cavernous
silence of unreason
colours bleed a crimson red
on streets of time and history's lanes

senses stand assaulted
a ravenous earth swallows
coffined loves
flames engulf countless pyres
hate conspires to feed the fires

stone-stoic chiseled eyes
of silent gods in sacred shrines
watch helpless the angry chaos
garden greens roar
a thousand war cries
vultures pepper the grey sky

healing notes from the mosques
restful chimes of temple chants
drown deep as echoes scream
roads turn pale in primitive fear
eyes blinded with stinging tears

a futile search for harmony
the moon shrouded in ignominy
stars lie scattered motionless
like wings of dying moths

the peepal tree in agony
witnesses countless broken memories
time's shadow dusted with ash
gasps and mourns
the countless gaping blackholes
that partition left behind.

60.

death is lighter than life

bound in the matrix
of miseries
tear-heavy eyes
mirror everyday shackles

an aching fragile mind
buried under shadows of despair
joins the stream of history
and pines for the other world
in its effort to silence life
tired listless winds fall silent
a quiet calm descends

with the approaching darkness
the solitary candle-flame
destined to die
flickers bright one last time.

neither body nor mind
not even the soul
wince under the weight
of lifelessness
for death,
is lighter than life.

61.

poet

the poet turns
wilderness to gardens
trapped sometimes
in the endless chaos
of life's aberrations
he implodes
in metaphor of time
in similes of dumb wrath
blind to truth
to light
to darkness
lost in the war of creation
and destruction.

62.

i shall change my questions

i walked the silence
of memory avenue
along quiet by-lanes
away from the bustling city of thoughts

the schoolyard comes alive
the shrine of childhood-city
thick lines and chalk-edged squares
define boundaries
for the much-awaited game
of hop scotch and jump

careful not to step on boundaries
i retrace the time-path
to priceless moments of togetherness
maneuvering flat pebbles
across squares, in earnestness
to reach the winning square

in this secluded memory lane
each square reflects laughter
laughter that mirrored
a thousand stars
why did you join the passing winds

my friend?
why do i constantly perceive bereavement
in the stillness of my universe?
why do the pink chalk-marked squares
assume the colour of death?

i never get to know the answers
so perhaps henceforth
i shall change my questions.

63.

mask

a house on the river
waves lap at the door
red grass smiles tall
sunrise brush-strokes paint purple
diamonds glitter
on noon's proud chest

sail boats on desert dunes
radiant peacocks open petals
winged dahlias in twilight bloom
gardens grow on verdant clouds
earth bathes in a rain of stars
nights burn in silver showers

smiles sketched in shadows of fear
infinity in finite's womb
chirping birds perched on the moon
rainbow across the night sky

all unseen, all unheard,
beneath, the masked surface.

64.

baba

disturbed dreams
rise from ruins of sleep
dark walls close in
i cling to my aloneness

burning incense sticks
stand lyrical, beside
fragrant flowers
as baba's eyes gaze through
the sandalwood frame

today time separates us
today we inhabit dual worlds
disjoint
but every night
he comes to me
as a silent tear.

65.

surrender

holding rusted memories
in my palm, i look into
the mirror of my poems
the mirror smiles away my lament

a second look
into the mirror and
i smile away the mirror's lament
of time racing past
leaving only a barren trail
and an empty horizon behind

i, my poem and a new emerging i
now grief, solace and strength
resume our search
for a slice of happiness
only to dissolve
in the flow of life
alongside barren lands

a thousand moons hence
we continue to remain
the progeny of time.

66.

peace is an eternal journey

distant sea-gulls
trace the homeward path
across silent skies, boundless
above the silver expanse, infinite
draped in swathes of tranquillity
harvest of peace!

desert-scape of thoughts
sense of reality lost in
rocking rhythms of nature
soulful brush-strokes of quiet calm
on the mind's canvas
oasis of peace!

rose and marigold petals
at the temple door and
the embrace of a thousand gods
harness the pace of time
it stands still for a while
folded hands, bowed head
metamorphosed sensitivity!

hushed chorus of burbling brooks
rustling leaves, the sailing breeze
time wades through autumn leaves

in soft footfalls
dreams wake up to the
salutation of quietude!

overcome by a finite sense
of completeness
realization dawns that
peace is not just a road
nor a direction
peace is an eternal journey.

67.

stones too can smile

the riverside rock
bemoans its mute existence
dry days lie in tatters
uncertainty lurks behind
iron-black nights

through deep shadows in its eyes
the mute stone watches
the riverbank come to life
as lovers nestle
under the canopy of darkness
between walls of the winds

poetry in every pause!

burbling waters in mica shine
wind their way
past the weather-worn stone
touching teasing
sometimes mocking

time arrives, beckons, summons
in a momentary lapse of reason
the surface-calm stoic stone
obliges time

obliges the turbulence within
and uproots itself
to embark upon
its course of destiny

forging desires, it races ahead
unsheathing its confused dignity
in unflinching faith, in secret indulgence
it surges past abstract paths
and narrow by-lanes
beating the winds
overstepping fuzzy lines between
reality of illusion and
illusion of reality
in search of new land
a land where
stones too can smile.

68.

language

an infinity of images
make a language
myriad colours float in
from beyond boundaries
from across oceans
like herons flying together
over endless waters
colours of traditional elegance
rituals, myth and history
map contours of cultures
their confluence with
the magnificence of centuries
touches the shores of the present
another language is born

distances close in, converge
thoughts leap
many frontiers, many eras
through flakes of time
they oscillate between
sleep and wakefulness
between the conscious
and subconscious

between real and surreal
with pristine poetry
nascence of yet another language

languages merge at the crossroads
connect with the cosmos
in absolute oneness
what emerges in poetic complexion
is the crowned queen of languages-
the universal language of
humanity.

69.

ashtray

they light
i burn in the richness
of intricate stonework
sometimes in crystal finery
absorbing everyday assaults
like a silent brick

entangled in ash dynamics
i am labeled
a dead millstone
cursed by my own fantasy
of bearing the eternal burden
of burning ash
as i watch the smoke of
drawing-room conversations
mingle with that of
burning cigarettes

but do not forget that
i house the ash that
depicts immortality
in ancient mythical treasures
for nobody can burn it
or destroy it

i rejoice in the depth of my being
as i remain the proud ashtray
that continues to house
the symbol of destruction
the symbol of permanence.

70.

elsewhere-land

the raft recedes
from the hammered land,
a screaming earth
and blood-raining skies

i leave behind my ripped roots,
the absent coherence
of a people
trapped in hissing flames,
in soot-black fog
of rising smoke
i leave behind the sinking earth
where evil-tainted wretched roads
lie buried beneath
sediments of human history

memory lingers awhile
before being swept away
by the tide of time

i seek refuge
in the ship's beckoning arms
as it sets sail
to the elsewhere-land,
the land of peace.

they opine...

• Dr Rita Malhotra's poetry collection Through the Prison of Time (Poems on Love, Hope, Journeys) celebrates the eternal existential battle of human spirit against the imposed township of inflected solitude. Her poetry magically describes the inner beauty of human resistance and resilience, through her powerful imagery in described human suffering, pain and failed relationships that bring grateful tears to the readers' eyes. Dr Malhotra, the poet and a friend, also paints beautiful, fragile and globalized pictures of love and dignity in many of her poems, including in the poems on Rembrandt's painting and on the self-portrait of Rubens. In her travel-poems, discovery of psychological belonging and historical dream-like description take over with poetic depth and charm.

—Dr. Amarendra Khatua
Former Ambassador and Secretary to
Government of India, writer and poet.

• Expressing very personal experiences in her poems, Rita Malhotra invents a language made of mathematics, physics, history, mythology, art and metaphysics - where Yama meets Rembrandt - giving a new glance on joys and sufferings of the "Venn Diagram of life": making an intimate music out of an encyclopaedic knowledge.

—Rolf Doppenberg
French Writer and Poet, Switzerland

• Rita Malhotra is a mathematician/poet. Every poem of Rita that runs on the super highway of abstraction finally resolves itself in a simple calculation. Desires and a hope merge themselves to an imagery that is truly Indian, words pulsate to a staccato of an unfolding sky immersed in colors, Rita Malhotra reigns the contemporary Indo English poetry scene.

—Amitabh Mitra
Poet, Artist, Publisher, Orthopaedic Surgeon
Editor "A Hudson View", 'Inyathi,'South Africa.

•   Professor Malhotra takes us on a journey in poems that draw upon the many complexities and contradictions that confront and confound our modern lives. She finds in these not only "the empty spaces of reality" but ultimately, and thankfully, "the train of reflections/ a touch of magic/ as the poetry lamp is lighted."

—Blaine Marchand,
Poet, Horticulturist and Former Diplomat,
Ottawa, Canada

•   Rita Malhotra is a poet of love of the genre of Kamala Das, albeit more restrainedand subtle and therefore powerful. Her aesthetic longing played in a tough game of chess; her cry for a violated girl; her love for the earth, water, air, sky and stars put her in the category of greatest contemporary women poets of Indian subcontinent. Her craft is that of a master sculptor who turns stone into a flawless figurine.'

—Anand Kumar,
Poet, Critic, Novelist,
Fellow of the National Academy of Medical Sciences
Professor and Head,
Department Of Reproductive Biology, AIIMS.

•   With great delight I read Rita Malhotra's poetry. Her poems are multifaceted: nature is omni present, but also love as well as the word, the poetic expression itself. She artfully mixes the actuality with philosophic reflections, unveiling her Indian roots which make her poetry even more fascinating for Western readers.

—Germain Droogenbrotdt,
bilingual Poet, Translator and Critic.

•   My introduction to Rita Malhotra was when I published the international poetry anthology 'Journeys.' Her intriguing words are honest and wise as a sunrise hastening the darkness to paint the dawn in beautifully vibrant kaleidoscopic colours of sad truths, love and hope.

—Graham Vivian Lancaster,
South-African Poet ,Critic, Editor "Journey".

•   Malhotra's poems, often compact, display what the American poet Robert Frost referred to as "a careful casualness." Her craft is very subtle and does not call attention to itself. Her observations are mature, pure and perceptive. It is through her poetic voice, honest, delicate, intelligent, individual yet universal that arrests the reader and leaves him or her with something truly profound and lasting.

—Peter Thabit Jones,
Poet,Critic and Editor "The seventh Quarry" Wales.

•   Rita's poems abound in philosophical wisdom as they transcend time and death. We get to see flowers and smiles, love and tolerance in her verse. She is a dedicated poet and a gift to the world of poetry.

—Hadaa Sendoo
Mongolian Poet, Editor W.P.Almanac,
World Poetry Ambassador to Mongolia and China.

•   Rita Malhotra is a poetess respected and admired by many poetry enthusiasts. Here once again she shares, her wealth of excellent poetry of all styles, covering so many different subjects. Her perspectives are truly inspiring and stimulating at the same time. Her poetry is sure to make a significant impact on the poetry world.

—Ashok Bhargava,
Poet, Economist, Founder Member,
Writers International Network, Canada.

•	Rita's poems reflect a rich and diverse variety of images that become symbols and metaphors, simple and complex; her conscious use of small letters everywhere with absolutely negligible exceptions, lend unique force to her themes and stylistic devices and rhythmic tunes and tones. All her poems are compact, compressed and short memorable lyrical pieces.

—Dr R.K.Bhushan,
Poet and Literary Critic,Former HOD (English) and Coordinator, Language, LPU, Jalandhar.

•	Dr Malhotra is very sensitive in poetic imagination with a certain abstract thinking in combination with deep concern about social reality. The poems have created a special impression in my mind while translating some of her poems into Chinese.

—Dr Lee Kuei-shien,
Taiwanese Poet, Critic and Translator.

•	Rita Malhotra's poems are unique, One of India's leading women poets, she travels the corridors of pain, painting the depths of sorrows with such beautiful words. She traverses the roads of despair, but weaves the sorrows gathered into hopes and dreams of a better although imperfect world.

—Ruth Wildes Schuler,
American Poet and Former Editor
"Prophetic Voices" Member, California Writers Club.

•	Rita Malhotra is one of the pioneers of Indian English Women's Poetry. The creative genius of Rita is chiefly visible in her poems of love, nature and man-woman relationship where she is both candid and confessional without any inhibition on her part and where she expresses her notions in simple, genuine and human style, displaying a rare emotional maturity, combining tenderness, passion and emotions. Her sensitive observations are both penetrating and piercing. Metaphoric images, graceful symbols, alliterative phrases, deed ruminations and excavations of heart's pain, fine arrangement of words, appropriate linguistic use, constitute her short poems.

—Dr.Shaleen Kumar Singh,
Poet, Critic and Editor "Creative Sapling"

•   Rita writes with freedom and courage besides also being comfortable in nature's embrace. From sighs to whispers, joys and pain her words touch a cord. She journeys into the inner world with her soft, precious and artistic skill to conjure up endless treasures of different emotions. Her lines are a boat across the river of life and her poems will live in our hearts until eternity. Rita flows through a world of words and like Annapurna feeds the soul with beauty like in her poetic line "I search for a poem in the wilderness of words."

—Stojomir Jamina,
Serbian Poet and Short Story Writer

•   Rita Malhotra is the immortal nightingale in the orchard of Indian English Poetry. Although she is a mathematician, her imagination soars high to provide Indian English poetry new heights of shades and zeal.

—Dr. Ram Sharma,
Poet, Critic, Faculty, English Literature.

•   For the mathematician, Dr. Rita Malhotra, life is a poem. Her poetic zeal is by no means an introverted affair, hence the recognition received.

—Sumit Talukdar,
Poet and Editor " Verse-Universe."

•   Rita Malhotra beautifully blends life's Mathematics with poetic rhythm. Her poems are graceful and emotive, especially her love lyrics which are marvelous, passionate and an open text of real life.

—The Pioneer.

•	Dr Malhotra's social consciousness, especially her concern for the girl-child and her deep anger at her plight are significantly reflected through her poems.

—Gurgaon Plus.

•	Dr Malhotra, as Former Principal of Kamala Nehru College, University of Delhi used her mathematical ability together with her poetic skills to keep the energy of the college on a heightened level and to maintain a balance between all stakeholders of the institution. She immaculately solves numerical equations and musically writes poetry.

—Delhi Diary, Vol 57

www.ingramcontent.com/pod-product-compliance
Lightning Source LLC
LaVergne TN
LVHW091000180726
843490LV00001B/358